AF578003

Questions?

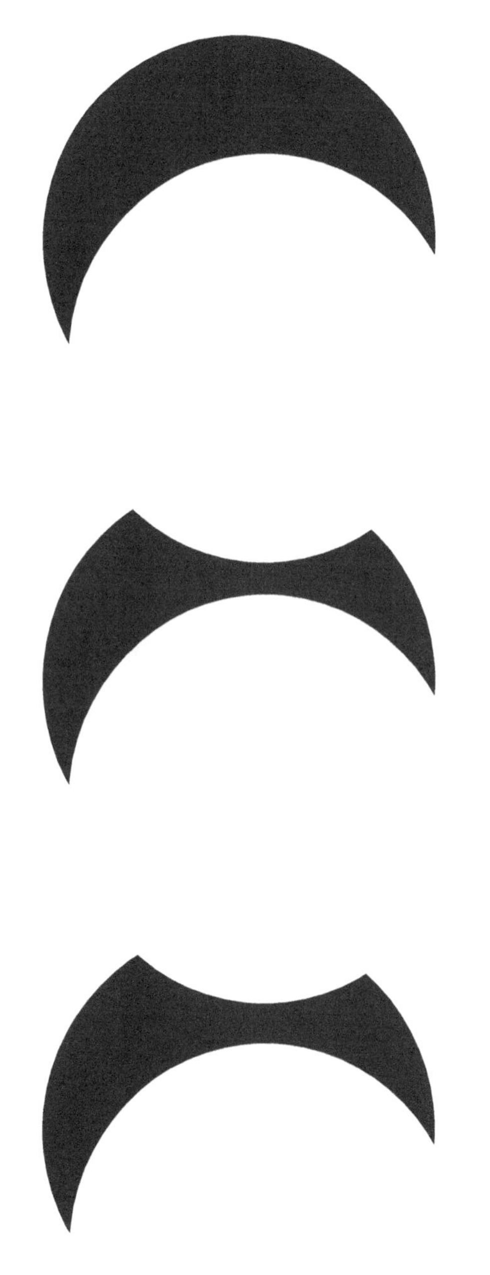

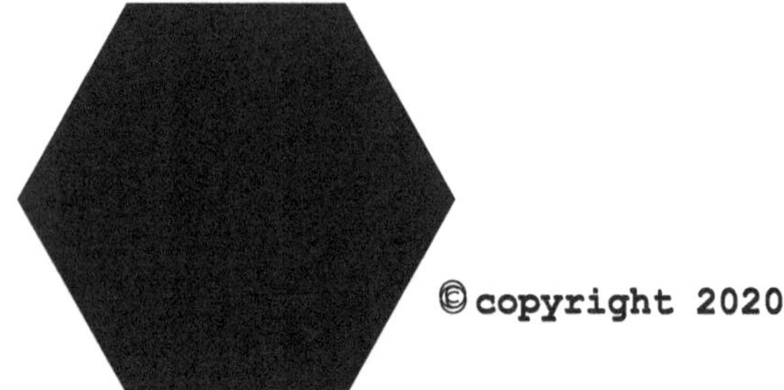

independently published

to those struggling with addiction
and
mental
illness

there is hope for recovery

"you don't have to live like that
anymore" -recovery quote

to M.C.
you were a star
in the dark sky
you planted seeds
in me
that have since
turned
into
flowers

in your memory,
i dedicate this first chapter

CHAPTER 1

TRANSITIONS

i continue
trying
to fill
this void

i try
to avoid
questions

people are always asking
like

are you okay?
what's going on?
are you going to be
alright?

well the voices in my
head
told me
that you
don't really
care
anyway

so what's the point in
talking?

seems like everyone is always
about the
chase
these
days

so they say

cut to the chase

    i know you live in
outerspace

        want to come over?
to my place?

i know what i should say
i should say
no
thanks

but there's something
about
the
way

i dread
the month
of may

so everytime i look
at
your face
i see his face
in
its
place

i know i'm
crazy
these days

we lost a good one
i remember you

you said i look
so pretty

i couldn't tell
you weren't
just saying that

wish i knew
then
what i know
now

i should've done more
i was so mean
i'm sorry for all that
i did
all that
i said

i want forgiveness
from
someone who is
gone

someone whose
voice
will
always be
in
my head

so many people say
i'm
so
lucky
i'm not dead

there are
so
many
nights
i wish
it was me
instead

you were a lighthouse
i remember
you

how could i
forget
all of the
things
we
went
through

a d d i c t i o n
is a battle
m o s t
won't survive

w e l l l l l l l l
i guess tonight is
the night
i will start
f e e l i n g
a l i v e

it's been
so
hard
since you
died..

i know your mom
still cries

your dad
still
tortures
himself
asking
why

your sister
deep in thought
with her successful
life

looks up
at
the sky
and wonders
why?

i often ask myself
i often ponder myself
what i could
have
done
differently?

could i have saved
your life?

t h e s e
q u e s t i o n s
t o r m e n t
me every night

i wanted to do something
for
you

because i know
how much
you meant

to everyone
who
considered
you
a
friend

i can't torture myself
anymore

so i put your
picture
in
a
drawer

i said
s o r r y
but there's no
l o v e
in my heart
anymore

i could’ve been so much
nicer
i didn’t realize

i didn’t know
what
real
pain
was

CHAPTER 2

SALVATION

i find it in my heart
to forgive

not because i need to
but because i have to

so many people can't
give
the
gift of forgiveness

i pretend i can't
hear
you

but

if i had
a chance
to react
to
those words
you pour
down my back
...

the darkness within me grows
everytime i go down
this road

i should say no
and
go home
while i still can

but

it's slipping out
of my hands

every last demand
just wanna get
a little more
high

just one more time

the voice says

t h i n g s
have changed but
i swear that
they will stay the
s a m e

maybe i should
be
ashamed
by all of the things
i'm
willing
to
throw
away

so now i’m granting
some
light
to everyone
i will
leave
behind

this feeling
inside my bones
they rub
together
like
two
stones

whether you can shake
it this feeeling
is here to
s t a y

while you're surrounded
by outward
displays
of madness

but you allow this..

i think about shit
sure
but that doesn't
imply
an
attachment to it

i read about shit
that doesn't
imply
that i
believe
it

i'm skeptical

by nature

s o m e t i m e s
i sense danger

meeting with strangers

well it's so wonder
I AM the thunder

i see myself
fall
a
few
rungs
down
the
social
ladder

you’d think
i’m 26
that it wouldn’t matter

i can't maintain
r e l a t i o n s h i p s
when i'm stuck like this

hunger pangs
set in
it's time again
to get right again

or take a nap...

i'm not complaining
i'm simply
explaining
that this is how
i feel
inside

CHAPTER 3

TEMPTATION

we live
in a world
where we are defined
by the ones
we keep at our sides

i deny
i'm one of them
but we party together
all night

i’m terrified
the
whole
time

worried that they’re spies

i do what i gotta do
to survive

o o o o o o o p s

i mean get
h i g h

i tell them
that
i'm not a thief

i have no children

who am i really hurting?

so am i the exception?

all i know is that

i want to give up
and say oh great
this is where
my life has gone

d o w n
t h e
d r a i n

my tolerance sets in again

oh great

or maybe
the dope
ain't that great

either way...

i have this pain
that i can't erase

i bite the hook
and pretend these
d a y s

---

all the pressure
i put
on
myself

to be
great

you'd think
if i just
put some
time aside
and looked
for the right
guy

...

you'd think
he'd remind me

but you see
we get weary
with those we
love

i don't have an olive tree
i don't own a dove

but this is my apology

written to you
with love

so the question
still remains

is this a higher
realm of consciousness
or
am i
fucking
insane?

voices in my ear
constantly
telling
me
things

can i believe what i see?
anger is not
b e c o m i n g
of me

i know one thing
though

i refuse
to
live
in fear

did you hear that?

CHAPTER 4

HESITATION

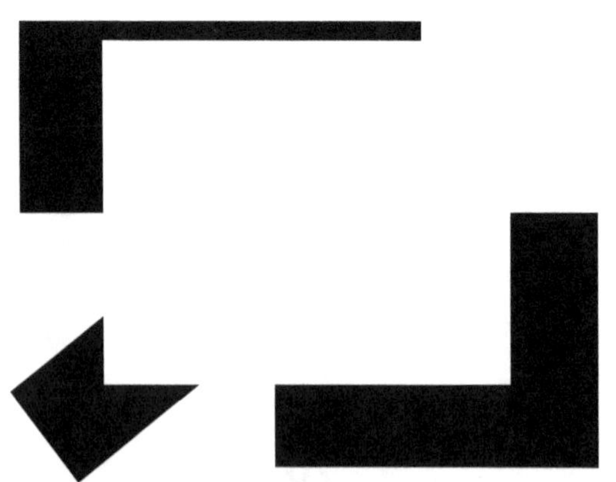

i feel like i don’t deserve
any of the
good things
that have been
happening to me

money
doesn’t mean
a thing
to me

this is what i crave:

freedom to study
freedom to travel
freedom to create

i will never
c o n f o r m
to their social norms

i won't let anyone
tell my that i'm
less than magical

now that the fever
dreams
i had
have passed

we know
nothing
in life
is made
to last

i can’t contain my thoughts
they’re so noisy
your voice and
the moonlight
soothe
me

i’m making
a decision
didn’t mean to hurt you

those weren’t my intentions

i didn’t mean to choose
the
wrong
move

now what do i do?
i'm looking all around for you

i don't know dude
i just choose to do
w h a t e v e r
i want to
with no regard
for you

i'm just a ship
in the ocean
keep waiting
for
an
explosion

but i’m wondering
what it’s like
to
be
perfect?

it’s like

you don’t even know
what
dirt
is

i can't stand this
time
of year

staying alive
for someone
else

doesn't seem fair

whether it be
p a s s s i o n
c o m p a s s i o n
take your time

never forget
the
pain
of
not being
able to
feel
anything

or feeling
too much

being numb is
to feel
as though
you cannot
grasp the sky
you can
slide
through
that narrow
space
in between
my eyes

it’s but a mystery
to be alive

as we are not born into
this
mental
slavery

when you have a free
t h o u g h t
you wonder a lot
a b o u t
where it came from

that's enough to make anyone
i n s a n e

so tell me
why are you
so sad?

there are great
times
ehead

rememeber the days
you couldn't
get
out
of
bed

you carry a burden
that's what
you
said

but there is no place
like my head
and no where
i'd rather be
than in bed

i try to find
some
reassurance

but

there's no way
out
of
my
head

CHAPTER 5

DAMNATION

what's up
with reality
these days?

it's like they're
putting
on
a
play

for mayhem and dismay

you see
i’m not
trying
to be
greedy
or hostile

i visit seedy
hotels
i sleep in my clothes
i need
something
for
my nose

all caught up in
it's throws again
and so i pretend that i can
dig my way out of it

if that’s a die
i guess
i’ll die

i’ll get
out
of
it

look quick
if you give me a hit
i'll sing you
my
misery

sweet in your ear
lullaby memories

i know you think
i'm crazy
however
we're just on
two
different
wavelengths

or are we on the same one?

we are all the son
of man
we are all
the sum of man

but please don't
shake my hand
g e r m s
scare me

i’m just trying
to
spin
it
in the most
positive
of lights

turn them off
if they’re
too
bright

if you're smart
you'll pack
your bags
lightly

i smile wildly
like a
coyote

because they will
never
own me

the molecular makeup
of materialism
is magnificent

but i spent every
last cent
indulging
it

now how will i make
r e n t ?
my house is so unkempt

i pray to god
for strength
and he sent me
y o u

i guess that's good enough
you know
i'm pretty tough
i'll make it through

what else can you do?

end your life contract?

better yet
establish
a
no
contact
order
with
the
past

start your life from scratch
create a new path
have lots of laughs
in your belly
eat lots of guava jelly

these drugs don't last long
u n f o r t u n a t e l y

i see myself
g o i n g
d o w n h i l l
but i can't stop

spent all night
hiding from invisible cops

i refuse to shop

i'm stretching out
i'm in my microcosm

i'm the universe
expressing
itself

i want to put
out
the
wildfire
in your
heart

if all i had to
give
you
was
one
word

it would be

resilliency

it's something
we desperately
n e e e d
in these times

i don’t want to live
like this

but i don't
want
to
die
like
that

CHAPTER 6

SITUATION

i prefer that my memory
be
left intact

instead
i have become
a placemat

if it's timeless
does it exist?
if so
can we reverse this?

i promise
i'm not trying to make
a political
statement

i just want to say this
...

those who cause us to
d i v i d e
want us to collide

they spiked the punch
with
cyanide

they put chemicals
in
the
sky

so many people
wondering
why

i can't decide

i have eyes
that widen
at the sight
of diamonds

but
i'm detoured
by their
sourcing

i eat liquid
m o r p i n e
for breakfast

what i’m trying to state
is that
i contemplate
life
for
days
at
a
time

without saying
five words
to
anyone

so let me
explain
to you
the
important
of
atiitude

c o n t r o l
the man on the moon
get him to
do whatever
you want him to

with
your beauty
simply

while corporations
profit
from
your
binds and ties
they keep you complacent
with
outragour
outright
lies

but still so many
wonder why
perfect
beings
are
idealized

i make another
declaration
i stare
into
the
headlines
of another
time

looking for patterns..

i glide on the rings
of saturn
but let me guess
that doesn't matter?

there's nothing you
can
tell
me
that i won't believe
because i've seen
a
thing
or
two
or
three

what do we
do
with
our
broken?
why
do
we make
jokes
about
them

it's better to
be a
friend
and lend some
time
to
spend
giving them
a hand

now let me state
to you
e v e r y h t h i n g
you view is stored
in your brain for
f u t u r e
u s e

now i’m scraping the pipe
another
sleepless
night

i don’t
want
to be there
but i don’t
want
to be here

i ran a fever
and it
made
my
mind
clear

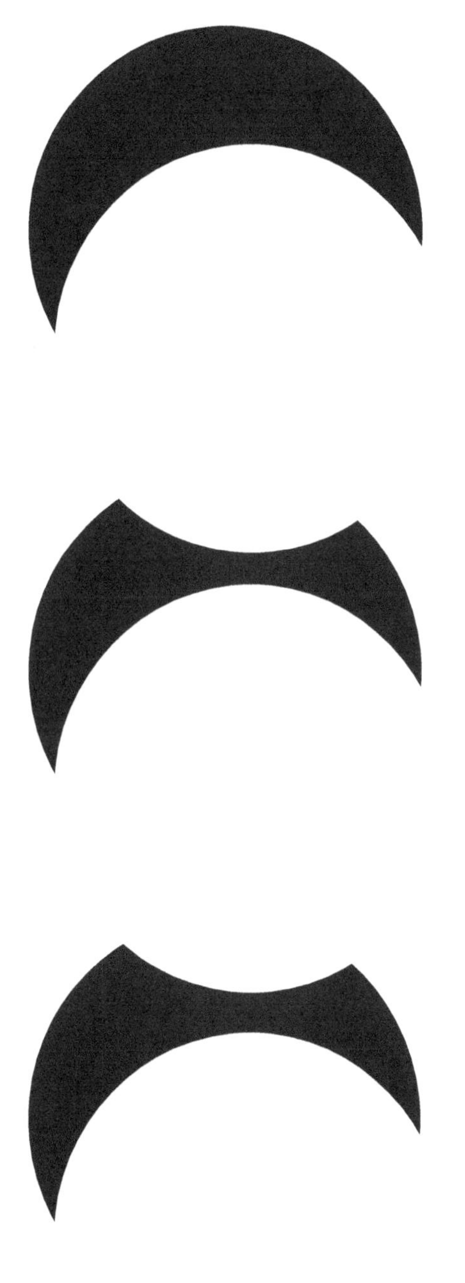

www.ingramcontent.com/pod-product-compliance
Lightning Source LLC
LaVergne TN
LVHW010606160826
845677LV00013B/3280

* 9 7 9 8 5 7 3 4 6 1 1 2 0 *